I SPY
A LION

— Animals In Art —

For my family

F O R E W O R D

A child looks at a painting and responds instinctively. As we grow up, many of us forget how to do this. Our children can help us to remember how to see clearly, and we can encourage them never to lose confidence in their own judgment.

My own children helped me to choose the pictures in this book and the animals to spy. I hope you will like them all, and that one day you may experience the thrill of seeing the original works of art and of discovering in them some familiar faces.

Lucy Micklethwait, 1994

I SPY
A LION

— Animals In Art —

Devised & selected by Lucy Micklethwait

Greenwillow Books, New York

I spy
with my little eye

a dog

I spy
with my little eye

a cat

Utagawa Hiroshige, *Asakusa Ricefields during the Cock Festival*

I spy
with my little eye

a mouse

Jan van Os, *Fruit and Flowers in a Terracotta Vase*

I spy
with my little eye

a rabbit

Titian, *The Virgin with the Rabbit*

I spy
with my little eye

a horse

I spy
with my little eye

a squirrel

Hans Holbein the Younger, *A Lady with a Squirrel and a Starling*

I spy
with my little eye

a lamb

I spy
with my little eye

a brown
cow

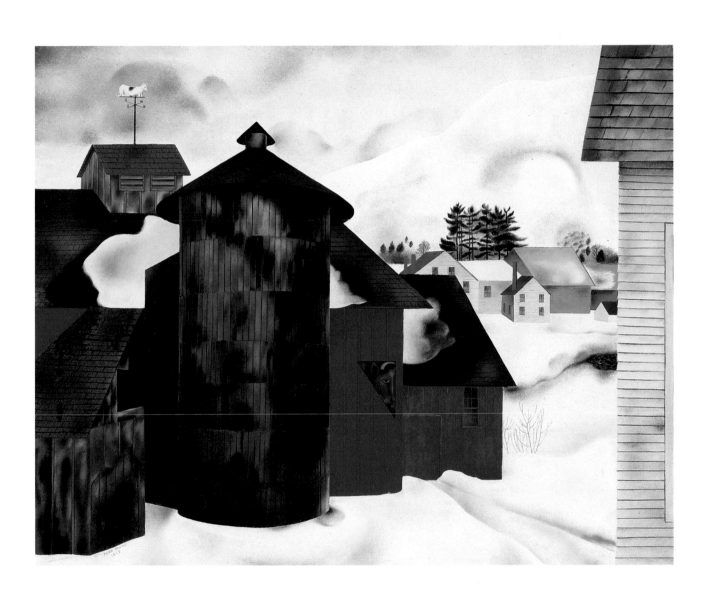

I spy
with my little eye

a parrot

Lucas Cranach the Elder, *Cardinal Albrecht of Brandenburg as St. Jerome in his Study*

I spy
with my little eye

a pig

Marc Chagall, *The Poet Reclining*

I spy
with my little eye

a goat

François Boucher, *Spring*

I spy
with my little eye

a tortoise

After Hieronymus Bosch, *The Concert in the Egg*

I spy
with my little eye

a snake

I spy
with my little eye

a lion

Henri Rousseau, *Representatives of Foreign Powers Arriving to Hail the Republic as a Sign of Peace*

I spy
with my little eye

a baby
monkey

I spy
with my little eye

a crab

I spy
with my little eye

an elephant

English, *The Animals, made on the Sixth Day of Creation*

I spy
with my little eye

a camel

August Macke, *Landscape with Cows and Camel*

I spy
with my little eye

a dragon

Bernardo Martorell, *St. George Slaying the Dragon*

I spy
with my little eye

two tigers

What do you spy?

Edward Hicks, *Noah's Ark*

I Spied with My Little Eye . . .

dog
Auguste Renoir (1841–1919), *The Luncheon of the Boating Party* (1881)
The Phillips Collection, Washington, D.C.

cat
Utagawa Hiroshige (1797–1858), *Asakusa Ricefields during the Cock Festival* (1857) from the series *One Hundred Famous Views of Edo*
Fitzwilliam Museum, Cambridge

mouse
Jan van Os (1744–1808), *Fruit and Flowers in a Terracotta Vase* (1777–1778)
The National Gallery, London

rabbit
Titian (about 1488–1576), *The Virgin with the Rabbit* (1530)
Musée du Louvre, Paris

horse
Fernand Léger (1881–1955), *The Great Parade* (1954)
The Solomon R. Guggenheim Museum, New York

squirrel
Hans Holbein the Younger (about 1497–1543), *A Lady with a Squirrel and a Starling* (about 1526–1528)
The National Gallery, London

lamb
Jan Steen (1626–1679), *The Poultry Yard* (1660)
Mauritshuis, The Hague

brown cow

Peter Blume (1906–1992), *Winter, New Hampshire* (1927)
Museum of Fine Arts, Boston, Bequest of John T. Spaulding

parrot

Lucas Cranach the Elder (1472–1553), *Cardinal Albrecht of Brandenburg as St. Jerome in his Study* (1526)
The John and Mable Ringling Museum of Art, Sarasota, Florida

pig

Marc Chagall (1887–1985), *The Poet Reclining* (1915)
The Tate Gallery, London

goat

François Boucher (1703–1770), *Spring* from *The Four Seasons* (1755)
The Frick Collection, New York

tortoise

After Hieronymus Bosch (about 1450–1516), *The Concert in the Egg* (16th century)
Musée des Beaux-Arts, Lille

snake

Attributed to Isaac Oliver (died 1617), *Rainbow Portrait of Queen Elizabeth I* (about 1600)
Hatfield House, Hertfordshire

lion

Henri Rousseau (1844–1910), *Representatives of Foreign Powers Arriving to Hail the Republic as a Sign of Peace* (1907)
Musée du Louvre, Paris, Picasso Bequest

baby monkey

Indian, Mughal School, *Lady Holding Strings of Pearls* (about 1760)
The Victoria and Albert Museum, London

crab

Pablo Picasso (1881–1973), *The Soles* (1940)
Scottish National Gallery of Modern Art, Edinburgh

elephant

English manuscript, *The Animals, made on the Sixth Day of Creation*
from *The Ashmole Bestiary* (about 1210)
The Bodleian Library, Oxford

camel

August Macke (1887–1914), *Landscape with Cows and Camel (1914)*
Kunsthaus, Zürich

dragon

Bernardo Martorell (about 1400–1452), *St. George Slaying the Dragon*
(about 1438)
The Art Institute of Chicago,
Gift of Mrs. Richard E. Danielson and Mrs. Chauncey McCormick

two tigers

Edward Hicks (1780–1849), *Noah's Ark* (1846)
Philadelphia Museum of Art,
Bequest of Lisa Norris Elkins (Mrs. William M. Elkins)

ACKNOWLEDGMENTS

The author and publishers would like to thank the galleries, museums, private collectors,
and copyright holders who have given their permission to reproduce the pictures in this book.

Utagawa Hiroshige, *Asakusa Ricefields during the Cock Festival*,
photograph © Fitzwilliam Museum, Cambridge.

Jan van Os, *Fruit and Flowers in a Terracotta Vase*;
Hans Holbein the Younger, *A Lady with a Squirrel and a Starling*,
reproduced by courtesy of the Trustees, The National Gallery, London.

Titian, *The Virgin with the Rabbit*;
Henri Rousseau, *Representatives of Foreign Powers
Arriving to Hail the Republic as a Sign of Peace*,
photographs © R.M.N.

Fernand Léger, *The Great Parade* © DACS 1994,
photograph: David Heald © The Solomon R. Guggenheim Foundation, New York.

Jan Steen, *The Poultry Yard*, Inv. nr. 166, photograph © Foundation
Johan Maurits van Nassau, Mauritshuis, The Hague, Holland.

Peter Blume, *Winter, New Hampshire*
© The Estate of Peter Blume/DACS, London/VAGA, New York 1994.

Marc Chagall, *The Poet Reclining*
© ADAGP, Paris and DACS, London 1994.

François Boucher, *Spring* from *The Four Seasons*
© The Frick Collection, New York.

After Hieronymus Bosch, *The Concert in the Egg*,
photograph: Giraudon/Bridgeman Art Library.

Attributed to Isaac Oliver, *Rainbow Portrait of Queen Elizabeth I* © Lord Salisbury.

Indian painting, Mughal School, *Lady Holding Strings of Pearls*,
courtesy of the Board of Trustees of the Victoria and Albert Museum, London.

Pablo Picasso, *The Soles* © DACS 1994.

English manuscript, *The Animals, made on the Sixth Day of Creation*
from MS. Ashmole 1511, folio 6 verso, The Bodleian Library, Oxford.

Bernardo Martorell, Spanish (Catalonian), *St. George Slaying the Dragon*,
photograph © 1993, The Art Institute of Chicago. All Rights Reserved.

Cover picture: Henri Rousseau, *Representatives of Foreign Powers Arriving to Hail the Republic as a Sign of Peace* (1907).

Title page picture: August Macke, *Landscape with Cows and Camel* (1914).

Library of Congress Cataloging-in-Publication Data
Micklethwait, Lucy.
I spy a lion: animals in art /
devised and selected by Lucy Micklethwait.
p. cm.
ISBN 0-688-13230-8 (trade).
ISBN 0-688-13231-6 (lib. bdg.)
1. Animals in art—Juvenile literature.
2. Painting—Juvenile literature.
3. Visual perception—Juvenile literature.
[1. Animals in art. 2. Art appreciation.]
I. Title.   ND1380.M53   1994
758'.3—dc20   93–30017   CIP   AC